THE MAN
who couldn't wait

Written by Joann Scheck

Illustrated by Alice Hausner

LUKE 5; JOHN 13; MATTHEW 26—28; MARK 14—16;
LUKE 22—24; JOHN 13:18-21; ACTS 2 FOR CHILDREN

ARCH Books

COPYRIGHT © 1971 CONCORDIA PUBLISHING HOUSE, ST. LOUIS, MISSOURI
CONCORDIA PUBLISHING HOUSE LTD., LONDON, E. C. 1
MANUFACTURED IN THE UNITED STATES OF AMERICA
ALL RIGHTS RESERVED

ISBN 0-570-06056-7

Peter the fisherman, bold as can be,
loves to be out in a boat on the sea,
where the winds and the waves
may be wild and rough,
where a man must be brave
and a man must be tough.

One morning early he's tired from fishing;
    he sits with his empty nets, dreaming and wishing
Then Jesus calls, "Peter, push out from the shore.
    Lower your nets in deep water once more."

The nets hit the water, and quick as a wink
they are so full of fish that the boat starts to sink.

"Peter, come, Peter,"
calls Jesus again,
"from now on
I'll make you
a fisher of men."

So Peter starts working
with Jesus on land.
But this kind of work
he cannot understand.

Jesus teaches and helps.
He is strong; He is kind.
He makes a man see
who had always been blind.

The people all love Him.
They shout and sing praise,
"We'll make Him a King
            to the end of His days!"

"When Jesus is King," Peter thinks, "I will be
 the King's greatest helper!" But friends disagree.
"I'll be the greatest," shout Andrew and John.
 "I'll be. No, I'll be!" They fight on and on.

They argue and argue
    till Jesus, their King,
with a cloth and a pan,
    does a wonderful thing:
He kneels beside Peter
    and washes his feet.
Peter, surprised, jumps
    up from his seat.

"No, Lord. Oh, no!
Oh, how wrong it would be
for Someone as mighty as You
to wash me!"
Jesus, while washing, says,
"Peter, be still!
You don't understand now,
but later you will."

A king washing feet? It doesn't seem right.
Peter's mixed up. Then later that night,
while Jesus is out in a garden to pray,
soldiers come marching to take Him away.

"I'll save you," cries Peter.
"Don't worry. I'm here."

And swinging his sword,
he cuts off a man's ear.

But Jesus won't fight.
　　　　He says, "Peter be still.
You don't understand.
　　　　We're not here to kill.
Now put down your sword.
　　　　Let the soldiers come near."
Then Jesus leans over and puts back the ear.

Jesus is captured;
    they take Him away.
He's nailed to a cross on a hill the next day.

Jesus is dead.
        His body is buried.
Peter is sad.
        He walks away worried.

Mary the third day
        runs into his room:
"Where did they take Jesus?
        He's gone from His tomb!"

Peter and John,
      as fast as they can,
run out to the garden
      and pass every man.

They find the tomb empty.
      Where can Jesus be?
They quickly return, the others to see.

Then Mary comes back, excited and glad:
"Cheer up, all of you;
now don't be so sad!
I've seen Him!
I've seen Him!
He's no longer dead.
He's alive!
He's alive,
just as He said!"

The men remain puzzled. "What shall we do now?
Jesus alive? How we wish it were true!"

Behind big locked doors each has a sad face
till later that night Jesus comes to that place.

He says,
    "Peace! I live.
Touch Me and see!
I'm not a ghost.
No need to fear Me."

He talks with them, eats with them,
many more times.

Then one day they're with Him when
up, up He climbs
to the top of a mountain.

He says,
"I must go
and return to My Father;
but now
you shall know
I'll send you My Spirit.
Keep watch till He comes.
He'll give you great power,
for you are the ones
to spread the good news,
to tell people of Me."
They watch
as He rises
until they can't see.

So Jesus is gone.
They're all alone now,
wanting to work
but not knowing quite how.
Peter stays with the others;
ten days they must wait
from morn bright and early
till evening quite late.

Then a roar fills the house like a wind rushing in,
    and flames shaped like tongues
on their heads can be seen.
    For Someone is there
           in this wonderful way,
Someone to help them
           in all that they say.

Peter jumps up.
    He cries out, "Now I see!
The Spirit of God –
        He is coming to me.
He's giving me power;
    He makes me feel bold.
I know what to do now.
    The world must be told!"

So Peter runs out unafraid, to the streets.
He stops and he talks to the people he meets.
"Give ear to my words.
The Jesus who died is alive and will save you.'
The crowd listens wide-eyed.

nd thousands who hear the good news of the Way
believe and are baptized that very same day.

DEAR PARENTS:

Peter is a real fisherman. He is strong, rough, and bold. One day he catches a boat full of fish because Jesus performs a miracle. He leaves his nets to become a disciple. He follows Jesus, hears Him teach, sees Him help people, observes His signs and wonders. Yet he does not fully understand Him. In moments of weakness he contradicts Jesus and even denies Him.

In the Upper Room he cannot understand why Jesus washes his feet. Jesus says, "What I am doing you do not know now, but afterward you will understand." He speaks of the Counselor, the Holy Spirit, whom He will send from the Father to teach all things.

Jesus' trial, crucifixion, and burial are even more difficult to understand. The appearance of the risen Lord renews Peter's hope, but he is still unsure and afraid.

Not after Pentecost! On that day the Holy Spirit descends on Him and the other disciples. Peter is a changed man after he receives the Spirit's power to go out on the streets and tell the crowds about Jesus, who died and rose again to save them from sin and death.

The annual Christian Pentecost festival celebrates this gift of the Holy Spirit. We hope the description of Peter's experiences helps you and your children understand the work of the Spirit.

The same Spirit comes to us through Baptism, the Gospel message, and Holy Communion. He dwells in us, giving us faith to believe in Christ and boldness to live for Christ and share Him with others.

THE EDITOR